3 — 11 — 14

From the Acorn of Discipleship...

Steps towards fruitfulness and personal growth

Revd. David Bedford

From the Acorn of Discipleship…

Onwards and Upwards Publishers

Berkeley House, 11 Nightingale Crescent, Leatherhead,
Surrey, KT24 6PD.
www.onwardsandupwards.org

ISBN: 978-1-910197-28-8
Typeface: Sabon LT
Graphic design: LM Graphic Design

Endorsements

David has walked the hard yards of pastoral leadership with integrity and energy, borne out of a deep spiritual interior. He earns the right in this book to offer a critique of the church he loves and to identify 'making disciples' as the main thing. It was back then and it should be today. I venture to suggest that any church leader not focusing on helping their people become a bit more like Jesus each day is missing the point.

Rev. Mark Elder
Senior Minister, Heaton Baptist Church, Newcastle

This short book is a very timely wakeup call about something that is vital to the church today - we urgently need to rediscover authentic discipleship if the church is to grow again and become effective in sharing the Good News of Jesus Christ. This is all about following Him, becoming active disciples and discipling others; people who are walking with God, under new management, transformed by grace and in the power of the Holy Spirit. In these insightful reflections from his Sabbatical, which include some very practical challenges at the end of each chapter, David dreams of a Church of passionate, fruitful, mature disciples making up a true community - filled with both grace and truth and with 'ragged edges'. He points out that embracing a renewed emphasis on discipleship will lead naturally to the church becoming more mission centred, helping others to become followers of Jesus.

Rev. Brian Harley
Chairman of GEAR, Group for Evangelism And Renewal within the United Reformed Church

From the Acorn of Discipleship...

About the Author

This book is the sum total of what the Lord reminded Revd. David Bedford of during his Sabbatical leave (March 17th to June 30th 2014) as a United Reformed Church pastor. The majority of it took shape as he walked, in its entirety, the 630 miles of the South West Coastal path over 48 days, and as he shared his thoughts with a Facebook group. David has been trying to follow Jesus since accepting Him as Lord and Saviour at a Boys' Brigade camp in Canada in August 1975, often failing in the flesh but by God's grace making progress in the Spirit. Trained in Manchester and Jamaica, he has had the privilege to lead and guide the life of many congregations in St Helens (1983-1987), Newham (1987-1992), Hastings (1992-1997), Guildford (1997-2006), Gosforth, Newcastle (2006-2012), and now in Canterbury.

A big turning point came in his life when someone he respected greatly asked him two questions: who is discipling you and whom are you discipling? Embarrassing or what? Ultimately he asked himself the question, 'What do I want on my gravestone: "Gone to another meeting" or "He helped twelve men follow Christ"?' In this book he seeks to help all believers in Christ become active, fruitful disciples themselves and at the same time disciple others. He believes that from the acorn of discipleship, once again can grow the oak tree of the Body of Christ.

CONTACT THE AUTHOR

Email: davidandlorna2012@btinternet.com
Phone: 07532 088253

I dedicate this book to Lorna, who has walked with me and with God.

Contents

From the Acorn of Discipleship…

Foreword by Ian Galloway

I'm glad to call David my friend.

I can't actually remember when we first met, but David's friendship to me has been life-transforming. I do remember the first time he called the five of us together, each of us pastors of quite different churches. Following David's call, we met every month for breakfast. We opened our hearts to each other. We held each other accountable and we cheered each other on. We laughed and we cried. We asked awkward questions and we prayed with encouragement and faith. It is a practice that continues to this day, despite David having now moved away. We simply added another friend. Life is better when you walk together.

David is a friend who is not afraid to challenge. He is in many ways a prophet to the church he loves. This book will get under your skin. It is neither comfortable nor comforting, but is a clear-sighted call to change. Its message is simple: put Jesus first in your life and then help others do the same. But the result of heeding David's call will be far-reaching. Putting open personal relationships and disciple-making at the heart of what it means to be a Christian will completely change you. It will also radically change the church, if enough of us can hear what the Spirit is saying.

David calls us to be full of grace, because without grace inviting people into your life can be dangerous. David calls us to be full of the Spirit, because making disciples isn't about offering each other self-help but connecting each other to God, who alone can change the heart. David calls us to mission, because being a Christ follower is not about introspection but seeking to be world-changing. David calls us to be mothers and fathers, because those new in the faith need patient and persistent love. David calls us to simplicity, because without radical de-cluttering of life you will never have the time or energy to disciple others with the consistency that is required. David calls us to community and friendship, because we find who we truly are when we are close enough to listen to those who love us.

David has a provocative message but he is no armchair critic. This book is from the heart of a Practitioner, a man who has been in the heat of the action for years. If you can hear his heart and see his vision,

From the Acorn of Discipleship...

you will be freshly energised in your faith. And, if you are willing to pay the price of not just hearing but doing, in years to come this will be said of you and your church community:

"They will be called oaks of righteousness, the planting of the Lord for the display of his splendour." (Isaiah 61.3)

It is the year of the Lord's favour.

Ian Galloway
Pastor
City Church Newcastle

INTRODUCTION

A Spiritual Elephant in the Room

I don't know about you but if there was an elephant in my room I think I would realise it! After all, it's not an ant, it's an elephant and can't really be missed unless I have closed my eyes to it...

As someone sincerely trying to follow Jesus in a post Christian and increasingly hostile culture, and as one who has sought to humbly respond to the Lord's call on my life since 1978 to be a pastor, I want to be honest in my assessment of where we are today as the UK Church yet faith-filled as to where we could and should be.

It is my conviction that the UK Church has largely lost its way because it has ignored the spiritual elephant in the room, namely discipleship. My friend Stephen Gibson in Mevagissey went as far as to say that most secular organisations pay more attention to discipleship than we do as the Body of Christ! The neglect and marginalisation of this central and core task of all who follow Jesus (Christians) has had a devastating effect on our congregations resulting in:

- New Christians falling away even after being Alpha-ised because no one has discipled them into maturity. No one is caring for these lambs, and left on their own they are falling away in great numbers; who will hear their cry?
- Children of Christian households falling away at an alarming rate (the majority of congregations now have no children) because they have not been discipled to face a hostile world and often see in their parents not committed disciples but slaves to a religious church culture.

- The classic historical denominational groupings in the UK (Anglican, Catholic, Methodist, Baptist, URC, Salvation Army) have all taken their eye off the ball of discipleship. All have declined, all aged – as many of my generation and younger have moved with their children to the 'New Churches' believing the spiritual grass to be greener – and, with some notable (mainly Baptist) exceptions, all are facing institutional meltdown.

- The 'New Churches' whilst giving discipleship more emphasis are far from getting this back into the heart of their congregations. Preoccupation with obtaining buildings, leadership issues including succession, and an unhelpful spirit of independency have sapped their spiritual energy.

- Optimistically whilst 59% in the UK would still claim to be 'Christian', the percentage actively/regularly connecting with a congregation is now as low as 7%; and whilst in London the trend is in the other direction, this is due mainly to immigration, leading to growing black-led and ethnic Pentecostal, and Catholic congregations. However 7% still represents around five million people in the UK; if we could only mobilise even 50% of these as a band of active mature disciples, the potential would be enormous!

'Religion' is given a tough time in this book, so it is reasonable to ask that I define what I mean clearly by this word. Those who are careless about their Christianity invariable get entangled in *sin*, whilst those who are careful and keen often get snared by *religion*. We begin our Christian lives with loving intensity, thrilled with God and committed to our relationship with Him. Sadly, that fervour can denigrate into a mere religiosity: we are passionate about our doctrines, opinions and traditions, and lose sight of the Living God in the process. The zeal is still burning but it is a religious zeal. Religiosity is a subtle enemy as well; it appears to be very pious and devout, but despite the disguise, religion is the sworn enemy of the Spirit of God.

So how can we bring about a new reformation in the UK Church and a subsequent return to fruitfulness? Answer: we can't but God can! The evidence of Church history amply demonstrates how much God desires to reconnect with His children, for in every generation there have been signs of a fresh outpouring from the Holy Spirit, calling the

Body of Christ to return to its missional task and its core activity of making disciples.

If this book seems harsh on my generation of church, it's meant to be, for I, along with all my brothers and sisters, bear some part of the responsibility for the demise of the church in the UK. However, I trust that what I have written, far from depressing you further, will be a small contribution towards turning the spiritual tide and a step towards redemption in the area of discipleship.

Acorns are tiny but from such grow huge oak trees. This book is my passionate plea to the UK Church to return to the acorn of discipleship from which I believe will flow and grow again the oak tree of mature and powerful Jesus-centred Christianity. The result of this would be that the UK would be reached afresh in a generation with the unchanging gospel of grace.

I trust that the Lord might allow my sojourn on earth to be long enough to see this.

David Bedford
Canterbury
2014

CHAPTER ONE

It says so in the Bible!

Discipleship is not an optional extra for the enthusiastic spiritual elite or for ministers/pastors paid to do such things. It's not cheap nor a quick fix nor another badge to wear; it's a lifelong journey and commitment. It's the Plan A strategy of Jesus for everyone who chooses to follow Him! Here's the good or bad news according to your perspective: there is no Plan B or C; that's it. When we do discipleship, Jesus does His bit and builds His Church; when we don't He has no building material (Matthew 16:18: '...I will build my church...' and Psalm 127:1: 'Unless the LORD builds the house...') with which to build.

The Great Commission (Matthew 28:16-20) has for most Christians become the Great Omission. Held up with the Great Call, to be witnesses to the ends of the earth (Acts 1:8), and the Great Command, to love God, one another, and our neighbours as ourselves (John 13:35, Matthew 22:37-39), these last words of Jesus on Planet Earth have become a badge to wear rather than a Jesus-shaped life to lead. Let's not, of course, look back with spiritual rose-coloured spectacles and forget that only eleven out of twelve disciples had graduated thus far, and all needed the baptism in and with the Holy Spirit, which would follow some ten days later. Even those gathered had doubts – these were very definitely saints with feet of clay – but such saints took the gospel to the ends of the earth in one generation. The Great Commission is addressed to disciples who had gone through an intensive one-to-one with Jesus and who had learned on the job what it meant to follow Him and do the things He did (Mark 1:17, John 14:12), but it is not just a call to *discipleship*. It's supremely a call to *make disciples*, and not just with your friends; it extends to every member of the human family.

Let's be honest...

Most of us have privatised our 'Christianity', claiming it to be a personal matter between 'me and God'. We have bought into a supermarket approach to faith, choosing only those aspects that allow us to maintain our comfort zone, and we have settled for a plastic imitation alternative called church.

Dietrich Bonhoeffer, one of my spiritual heroes said rightly that 'Christianity without discipleship is always Christianity without Christ.'[1] Don't you, like me, feel that what passes as following Jesus – the Sunday treadmill; the disconnect with my everyday life; the lack of power, vision and faith; the increasing irrelevance of what we do as Church to the people around us – is not what we signed up for?

How can we change?

Let's start with the Bible – what it says, more explicitly what *He* (Jesus) says – and drill down deep into the Great Commission. Let's be bold enough to ask why we are so powerless in the UK whilst a believer in China is making such an impact and seeing the transformation of a nation.

The first thing to note is that it is addressed directly to all disciples, including those who have made the choice to follow Jesus in this day and generation. Such a decision is one we make at the point of our conversion (becoming a Christian); the Bible suggests that this is a work of grace (we don't deserve it) by Jesus (who has paid the price for our sin and rebellion) who calls us and draws us to Himself (John 12:23).

> John 15:16
> *You did not choose me, but I chose you and appointed you [to] bear fruit – fruit that will last...*

We cannot make Christians; that's exclusively the work of God: the Father who created us, the Son who died for us (in our place), and the

---

[1] Cost of Discipleship (pp. 59, 89); Dietrich Bonhoeffer; Simon & Schuster (SCM Classics 2001)

Holy Spirit whose life and power is ours as we become 'new [creations] ... the old ... gone, the new [come]' (2 Corinthians 5:17). No intermediaries like your elder, priest or pastor – no one to blame! What we can do is to choose to follow Jesus and to be His disciple (no one else's) – and like most choices in the life of discipleship this needs to be regularly renewed and affirmed to Christ, to others, and to the unseen spiritual forces of darkness arrayed against the gospel and all believers.

The second thing that we not only miss but hugely underestimate is that Jesus says, 'All authority in heaven and on earth has been given to me.'[2] Some interpret that as Jesus giving the disciples a kind of delegated authority, and this leads into a kind of guru-led Christianity which is nowhere to be found in the pages of the New Testament. No, this authority which is total ('All') has been given to Jesus by His Father. When He walked Planet Earth He showed that He had authority over the natural order, sin, sickness, and death. Now such authority not only remains complete but, as He is occupying the Throne of Grace in His risen power, it's not even limited by His humanity. So if the authority extends over all humanity I'd do best not only to listen and follow but also to come of my own freewill under His authority. It also extends over the evil one (Satan or the Devil) and all his minions. Satan is the prince of this world, who still seeks to oppose God and His people, but who has been defeated once and for all at the cross and who is on parole until the day Jesus returns to Planet Earth and 'calls time' on all his worst efforts[3]. So we have no authority of ourselves, but we can exercise Christ's authority when we do the things He did and wants us now to do. 'In the name of Jesus' is not a lucky charm or magic words that we can utter to access Him; it is how we exercise His authority today. Similarly we can declare the completed work of the cross over sin, sickness and death.

Thirdly, Jesus says, 'Therefore go and make disciples of all nations.'[4] Whenever you hear the word 'therefore' you need to check what comes before it! Answer: nothing less than the Resurrection. We might think to ourselves: who am I to be about such a world-changing task? But be reassured: one who has all authority is commissioning us! Now whilst most Christians know the Great Commission by heart, a

---

[2] Matthew 28:18
[3] Read Revelation for the whole story.
[4] Matthew 28:19a

much smaller proportion move from being hearers of the word to being doers also (James 1:22). Why is that? Well one answer may be 'fear'; I am being told to go into a hostile world on my own, and even to the ends of the earth (Acts 1:8), and surely didn't Jesus send out disciples two by two? I have to say that I have some sympathy with this perspective and want to ask why translators have consistently translated the Greek 'Go', when it could as easily be also translated 'Come'. 'Come' sounds more like Jesus saying, 'Come with me and share in this amazing task of disciple-making.' 'Come' suggests the work of salvation has already begun and we are being strategically placed to disciple new converts and bring them to maturity. 'Come' has more of a 'two by two' feel to it, more of a partnership in the gospel context, and it sits well with the other 'comes' from Jesus (John 1:39, Mark 1:17). Perhaps it could be translated, 'In your comings and goings make...' The reason to go or come is to make disciples, which is so clearly a responsibility laid on all disciples then and now. Not an option, it's a command, and the measure to which you and I do this will be the measure of our fruitfulness. In the other chapters of this book we will look in more detail about what this might entail and why we have made this so difficult for ourselves, but for now let me say it is clearly something that is *intentional*. It doesn't happen by chance or osmosis; it's planned and clearly/prayerfully fitted to the individual's unique ('...your salvation...' – Philippians 2:12) journey of faith. Which leads me to 'of all nations' – or 'all ethnic peoples', as the Greek suggests. Later I will share about us each having our own unique mission fields but suffice it to say here that we need to, with the Holy Spirit's help, work out what the gospel means to every unique people group in every context, and help them to follow Jesus in a way that does not alienate them from their culture but gives them ways of putting Christ above the culture and speaking into it and to their peers. The last thing we want is a re-run of the mistakes made by early missionaries in Africa, Asia and America, where they failed to separate so-called civilisation and the Empire from rooting the gospel in the places where people were.

Next we are told that as disciples we should be 'baptizing them in the name of the Father and of the Son and the Holy Spirit'[5]. Hey now,

---

[5] Matthew 28:19b

here's a revolutionary thought: *you* disciple them, *you* baptise them! No mention of sacramental ministry here or the necessity of having the church leader present. Also note that this is clearly speaking of those who have chosen to follow Jesus and become His disciples, so those old enough to make that choice/decision. There is of course an important part played by the local gathering of believers to ensure someone is ready for baptism although my own experience and conviction would suggest that we should not place hurdles (especially non-biblical ones) in the way, nor should we delay baptism long after conversion (it is after all an immediate response to the preaching of the gospel). Romans 6 encapsulates what baptism is:

> Romans 6:3-4
> *Or don't you know that all of us who were baptized into Christ Jesus were baptized into his death? We were therefore buried with him through baptism into death in order that, just as Christ was raised from the dead through the glory of the Father, we too may live a new life.*

When the Church was born on that first Pentecost, the process was fivefold (Acts 2:38-47): repent, believe in Christ, be baptised, receive the Holy Spirit, and join the Church. A good halfway house on baptism I use is to baptise with the person who is discipling the candidate, thus affirming their unique spiritual father/mother relationship and making the connection with the whole Body of Christ. We love to focus on secondary issues, one of which is infant baptism (and confirmation) or believer's/adult baptism. For years we have pushed the very personal heart of baptism into the shade as we have nit-picked over the relative theological merits of how, when and to whom it should be administered. Ultimately the form is not as important as the reality of the believer following Christ and being a disciple for the rest of their temporary sojourn on Planet Earth. It is helpful, however, whatever form is used, to get all present to re-affirm their own baptism, to get the candidate to share their story of faith (testimony), and to focus prayer on, support and actively disciple the newly baptised.

Then Jesus tells us that in the disciple-making process teaching is all-important, just like the teaching[6] that had been given to the twelve – and its reasonably specific teaching too: '[the new disciples must]

---

[6] The Greek verb for 'disciple' also translates as 'teach'.

obey everything [He has] commanded them.'[7] I can hear the murmurs and the protests: 'Privatised Christianity strikes again! Don't you tell me what to do!' So what did Jesus command? Well, we have already mentioned the Great Commission (spoken out of 'all authority'[8]), the Great Call (a command with a promise of 'the Holy Spirit'[9]) and the Great Command (to love God, one another and neighbour). That would do for starters but then add in the Ten Commandments (Exodus 20:1-17) affirmed by Jesus, which seem pretty tame compared to the interpretations added in the Sermon on the Mount (Matthew 5-7). Someone also once commented that if we would take seriously all the 'one another' commands in scripture, revival would break out overnight! Now let's remember these are not additional pharisaic rules or extra-biblical church requirements most of which have no place in a disciple's life; they are from Jesus, and they are showing us a new way of Kingdom Living which is as relevant today as it was 2000 years ago. This teaching needs to happen in one-to-one discipleship, carefully in small groups and systematically from the pulpit.

Let me just mention one other tricky word at this point, which is biblical and has been crucial to my maturing as His disciple: *submission*. Three aspects of this need to be grasped: firstly, 'Submit yourselves, then, to God. Resist the devil, and he will flee from you.' (James 4:7); secondly, 'Submit to one another out of reverence for Christ.' (Ephesians 5:21); and finally, '[Obey] your leaders and submit to their authority...' (Hebrews 13:17). Sub-*mission* is what undergirds the very *mission* of the Body of Christ; we ignore it, and maintain our independence, at our peril!

The final sentence of the Great Commission is known by all and has become like the veritable Christian comfort blanket: 'And surely I am with you always, to the very end of the age.'[10] Now forgive me if this seems cruel, like yanking the comfort blanket away from your comfortable pew, but like all scripture we need to see this promise in its context and as conditional upon you and me fulfilling to the best of our ability the charge to make disciples. Am I suggesting that the promise is works-dependent? No. But I am saying that it's the fruit of

---

[7] Matthew 28:20a
[8] Matthew 28:18
[9] Acts 1:8
[10] Matthew 28:20b

obedient discipleship. Jesus clearly sets out the cost of discipleship, and on that basis we choose obediently to follow or not (Luke 9:57f). There appears to be no place for half-heartedness. Do it and He will be with you; don't and why indeed would He rubber-stamp your disobedience? Again this sits well with the 'go' or 'come' debate: if He is going to be with me always then it feels more like a 'Come!' Oh, and I love the 'always' bit as it reminds me of 2 Corinthians 9:8:

> *And God is able to bless you abundantly, so that in all things at all times, having all that you need, you will abound in every good work.*

No mere comfort blanket, it's the Saviour of the world helping you realise your eternal destiny! So read again this Great Commission, and be and make disciples.

Matthew 28:16-20
Then the eleven disciples went to Galilee, to the mountain where Jesus had told them to go. When they saw him, they worshiped him; but some doubted. Then Jesus came to them and said, 'All authority in heaven and on earth has been given to me. Therefore go and make disciples of all nations, baptizing them in the name of the Father and of the Son and of the Holy Spirit, and teaching them to obey everything I have commanded you. And surely I am with you always, to the very end of the age.'

Acorns to oak trees: 3 steps towards mature discipleship

- Find someone whom you admire and respect spiritually, and ask them to disciple you.
- At the same time ask the Lord to give you a new or young Christian to disciple.
- Take a long hard look at what you are doing and ask how much of it sits well with the Great Commission. Dare to read about the Church in China!

CHAPTER TWO

It does what it says on the tin!

Richard Halverson, former US Senate Chaplain, writes:

> *The Church began as a fellowship of men and women centred on Jesus. It went to Greece and became a philosophy. It went to Rome and became an institution. It went to Europe and became a culture. It went to America and became an enterprise.*[11]

When I read this quote recently, it resonated deep within me and I wept. In this chapter I want us to ask how we can return the Church to its pure roots so that it clearly does that which it says on the tin! I want to be part of a Church that is as attractive as Jesus, as relevant and real as His ministry, and because of that '[enjoys the favour] of all the people' (Acts 2:47). Such a Church would be full of people who are being and making disciples, and it would be without walls or boundaries. Just as there is no 'Plan B' for discipleship, there is no 'Plan B' for Church.

> Ephesians 3:10-11
> *His intent was that now, through the church, the manifold wisdom of God should be made known to the rulers and authorities in the heavenly realms, according to his eternal purpose that he accomplished in Christ Jesus our Lord.*

Let's be honest...

Richard Halverson is correct in his assessment. We have taken the pure, spotless, unadulterated Body of Christ and thought that we could

---

[11] http://timpanogos.wordpress.com/2009/01/20/quote-of-the-moment-richard-halverson-chaplain-of-the-us-senate/

do a better job than the only head of the Body, our Lord Jesus. We have made the word 'Church' a big turn off; it's become synonymous for old, cold, unfriendly buildings of bricks and mortar rather than living stones. It used to be somewhere you went for rites of passage (baptism / christening, weddings, funerals) but now people don't even think about having their babies 'done'. Weddings (if they happen) take place at more glamorous and less formal locations, and funerals take place directly at the crematorium, cemetery or woodland burial site. If people do see Church as the People of God they assume we will judge them. 'Unchristian: what a generation really thinks about Christianity, and why it matters' by David Kinnaman[12] was based on a survey of twenty- to thirty-year-olds (half Christian and half not) about Church in America. It found that there was very little difference between the two samples. Over 85% thought Church / Christians were judgmental, hypocritical and homophobic.

How can we change?

Let's be bold and give Jesus His Church back and stop thinking we know better! Let's be bold enough to try to return as Church to our core calling and function: making disciples. I am not primarily interested in philosophy, culture, institution or enterprise. I simply want to be a disciple and to make disciples, to follow Jesus as best I can today, and to do this with others.

Lord, please give us another chance to get this right in the UK – have mercy! I want to be part of a Grace Community, a Church with Ragged Edges, where no-one apart from Jesus defines who is, or is not, part of His Body!

Whilst walking the South West Coastal Path I was thrilled and fascinated with Cornwall's Christian history; saints abound, and the Methodist revival in the late 18th century made a real and lasting impact amongst ordinary people with John Wesley visiting thirty-eight times. Wesley developed a simple methodical plan for maturing and equipping the saints. Four basic convictions underlined his approach: the necessity of discipleship for every Christian, the place of small groups, leadership was essential (1 in 10 were made leaders), and that holiness and service were the goal. Small groups had three levels:

---

[12] Published by Baker Books

Societies (congregations for the crowds), Classes (like Cells, mirroring Jesus' twelve and for both sexes with all speaking honestly and openly) and Core groups (of four of the same sex, who opened themselves to each other in a totally accountable and confidential way).

Now, however, wherever you turn you will find closed or converted chapels or churches. How could a movement with such an effective method of discipling men and women lose its way so profoundly? Generally the answer is that every generation must rediscover what it means to follow Jesus. In this case, by 1830, two generations after Wesley's death, the class system in the UK had fallen into disrepair; energy was then put into building bigger buildings and competing with different brands of Methodism (Primitives, Bible Christians, Wesleyans). So when in the 1850's God raised a young firebrand up called William Booth, Methodists had settled so significantly they could not cope with him and the Salvation Army was born! Since then Methodism has become almost the most minister-centred, rule-based grouping within the UK Church!

An example of how some find the church difficult came from friends in Cornwall who would describe themselves as Christians trying to follow Jesus and who are in vital jobs in the education system (headmaster and teacher). They have given up on 'Church' because 'it's rule based, demanding, judgmental and just not helping [them] follow Jesus'. What a sad indictment!

The problem seems to be that as Church we have become building- or institution-centred rather than people- or community-centred, and discipleship-focused. This needs to be addressed and hopefully gradually changed if we are to truly be once again salt and light for our nation and to the ends of the earth.

The New Testament has many revealing emphases that we need to heed and act upon. For instance, the word 'Christian' is only mentioned three times but 'disciple' appears 269 times – so what is that saying to you and me? The word 'Church' is also only mentioned three times (Ephesians 3:10, Matthew 16:18 and 18:17[13]) whereas 'The Way' is mentioned five times (Acts: 9:2, 19:23, 22:4, 24:14,22) and, of the many descriptions, 'Body' is the most memorable and prominent.

---

[13] This passage teaches about Church discipline

From the Acorn of Discipleship...

'The Way' points us to one on the move (Jesus) and suggests that we need to follow and have His attitudes (Matthew 5:1-10, Philippians 2:5), do the things He did (John 14:12), be generous (2 Corinthians 9:6b), prayerful, prophetic, full of grace and following the way of 'agape'[14].

'The Body of Christ' is an even more profound metaphor. Again, bodies are for movement not to be static; don't move and you will eventually seize up! Jesus being the head of the Body underlines that without Him there is no body. You can cut off or amputate many other parts of the body, but cut off someone's head and that's it. Every part of the body, large or small, seen or unseen, has a unique role in its overall function. Jesus had a unique ability to draw people to himself, without judgment, and to respond to where they were at; so the Body of Christ too should be the face of grace to a world searching for meaning and answers. As someone once said, 'A world falling apart needs to see Christians coming together.'

The definition of the word 'Church' has become confused, with people using it to describe their unique attempt to gather Christians, but the truth is that there is but *one Church* with *many congregations* and it's called the Body of Christ. I believe that God is calling a halt to our spiritual trivial pursuits and wants to remind us of the prayer prayed by His Son when he cried, 'Father may they be *one*... so that the world may believe' (John 17:21, emphasis added). Disciple-making would become a whole lot more achievable if we were *one* as we would have the 'commanded blessing' of Psalm 133:3. Of course the enemy of our soul does not want us to 'do what it says on the tin' as the body of Christ. He delights to see us struggle to maintain institutions local and national, too heavy and expensive and achieving little. He hoots with unholy laughter when he see us using models of church and ways of worshipping which weren't working twenty five years ago. He rubs his hands when we spend 95% of our income on our buildings and professional clergy and only 5% on mission and discipleship!

Will our protestations when we appear before the judgement seat hold any sway? 'Well, Lord, it was our pastor. If only he had done better...', 'Well, Lord, it was that horrible building we had; it took all

---

[14] Agape is the Greek word that points us to God's perfect love embodied in Jesus.

our energy...', 'Well, Lord, we wanted to do things differently but denominational rules said...'

If buildings are coming before people then we need to find a way to change that. One congregation that I visited in Dawlish had created a separate trust to look after their building and because the trust (which is wider than the congregation) is not a church it can attract grants to upgrade the facilities. The congregation now uses the space as before but pays the trust for such use without having the blank cheque of looking after the buildings themselves. They say that it has released them to concentrate on their core task of worship and making disciples. Could this be rolled out elsewhere as a similar model? I hope so.

If institutions are coming before community then the institutions, both locally and nationally, need to see this folly and act. Given that certain functions must be done, practically and legally, could not smaller congregations be grouped together as one legal entity? We need to do all we can to encourage this transition back to being the living, loving growing organism called the Body of Christ that lives its life to a different drumbeat to the world around it, and in such a way that spells HOPE, shows JESUS, and values people.

Why? Because that's what it says on the tin called Church!

Acorns to oak trees: 3 steps towards mature discipleship

- Ask yourself whether your focus is on church or on being and making disciples? Resolve to rethink your priorities.
- Encourage and pray for your leaders to be brave enough to set aside a season to look at your life together as a congregation and seek to return to your core tasks and as Church do what it says on the tin!
- Again pray about and encourage your leaders to consider different ways of running and funding your buildings so that the lion share of your resources go on mission and discipleship.

CHAPTER THREE

It is all a matter of good parenting

Isaiah 54:1
'Sing, barren woman, you who never bore a child; burst into song, shout for joy, you who were never in labor; because more are the children of the desolate woman than of her who has a husband,' says the LORD.

I'd love to have called this book 'It's not over till the barren women sings!' But I guess that the title would be lost on most people. Here Isaiah speaks out prophecy over the nation of Israel. In essence, God doesn't see His people as barren; He sees them as fruitful, so then Israel – and we today no less – can rejoice! Much of the church in the UK today is barren, and has been for a good while, but I believe that the Lord sees us as fruitful and that we not only need, with faith, to see the same but put in place the mission strategy laid out in the following verses (Isaiah 54:2f). Put simply: we make disciples when we *are* disciples; reproducing is our business.

Let's be honest…

The problem most of us have with becoming spiritual mums and dads is that we have struggled at the first hurdle with our own children. Many who have grown up in our congregations have not reacted well to our outdated ways of worship and communicating God's word, and poor models of working with children and youth. As soon as they have been allowed, Church has been kicked into touch as irrelevant and has often been seen as something that takes their parents away from them. Many of God's best saints have prayed over and sought to model Christ to their children, but to their great sorrow the children have either rejected the gospel or are indifferent. So how can we become spiritual parents?

How can we change?

Well we could start by not beating ourselves up and by resolving in our hearts to redeem not only our children but also many others who would be blessed by our parenting of them in Christ. Spiritual Parenting is not confined to natural parents, as many who are, or choose to be, single make amazing disciples and often have more time to invest into the lives of others in Christ. Let's accept the mess the Church has been in for a long while, that we too have been casualties of it, even if we have also been its silent architects. The Lord is gracious and compassionate, not only offering forgiving grace but a new faith-filled beginning.

Let's not think that discipling the next generation cannot happen, for it has and still does by God's grace: Lois to Eunice to Timothy ('fan into flame the gift of God') in 2 Timothy 1:6; and for me personally, I was prayed for by Nanny Nellie and Nanny Winnie, encouraged by my mum and dad and mother church, and then with Lorna we prayed and laid hands on both Megan and Lydia at their baptisms (now we pray for our granddaughter Isla Grace). It's all about passing the spiritual baton on, and times like baptisms and weddings are huge opportunities to do this. Interestingly, Mothering Sunday is the day when we are supposed to return to the congregation who nurtured us, but of course it was not a building or institution that did this but actual precious saints who cared, nurtured and discipled us.

As parents we have been through that steep learning curve of 'Help, I'm a parent!' and by the grace of God learnt to undertake one of life's biggest privileges, that of shaping and nurturing a young life – roots and wings. Therefore, with the help of the Holy Spirit it is not a huge jump to apply that to becoming spiritual mums and dads to many. Helping another soul follow Christ, discover their destiny, and make a difference on Planet Earth is probably second only to doing this with your own physical children. We all need role models in every aspect of our lives and no more so than in the realm of discipleship and following Christ. That's why we need to primarily 'work out your salvation with fear and trembling' (Philippians 2:12b).

Note that we can't work out anyone else's, much as we are tempted to do so! We can hopefully ensure that the model of discipleship we are displaying is worth someone imitating. How? By becoming discipled and accountable to another fellow disciple. In my experience this can happen to some extent through Christian Marriage (after all, that is a journey too into becoming one flesh), but it is also very effective when men are accountable to other men and women to women (2 Timothy 2:22).

Wesley's class system in its purest form was a way in which men were accountable, one to another, and it produced many giants of faith and servants of the Lord who took the gospel to the ends of the earth in the great missionary era. My own experience was enriched immensely when I and four other pastors in Newcastle met once a month on a Saturday morning at 8am for breakfast. Following the breakfast each of us in turn bared our souls with their successes, failures, challenges and frustrations. The others then questioned the one sharing with no area off limits. We then prayed for them and prophesied over them. When it was our turn we looked forward to it and it became a huge springboard for us all to grow and deepen our lives as we tried to follow Jesus. We also became very good friends because we lived intertwined lives. Interestingly, but not surprising, is the observation that the more I submitted/opened my life in an accountable way to others, the more effective and authentic I was in doing the same with others for whom I became a spiritual father.

Paul hints at this accountable relationship twice in 1 Corinthians.

1 Corinthians 4:15-16
Even if you had ten thousand guardians in Christ, you do not have many fathers, for in Christ Jesus I became your father through the gospel. Therefore I urge you to imitate me.

1 Corinthians 11:1
Follow my example, as I follow the example of Christ.

Should not all disciples be able to make such statements? The mention of guardians probably alludes to the church in Corinth, and in most local congregations today we tend with younger and new Christians to act like guardians – relationship at arm's length, care with strings, the smile or the frown, the positive response if they conform or negative if they don't. Fathering is much more relational, through thick and thin, hands on, and being prepared, like Jesus with the twelve, to walk with the person you are fathering for the long haul despite how many times they might mess up. 'Imitate me' or 'follow my example' is a huge thing to say to another soul seeking to follow Jesus, but what's the alternative for them: reading the Bible and trying to work out how to follow Jesus on their own? Discipling is therefore at the same time the most wonderful privilege and the most demanding task the Lord will ever give you, but it is the prime and supreme task for all believers without exception. When done well and effectively the results are amazing: fruitfulness, joy, a sense of destiny, and relationships for life. To see those whom you watched become Christians and helped disciple launched into the world, often married, making a unique impact, and then disciplining a new generation, gives you a buzz like no other. At this point, can I commend to you a read of 'The Imitation of Christ' by Thomas a Kempis?

Of course, relationship is right at the heart of not just discipleship but all effective evangelism, dynamic Christian community and fruitful ministry; all stemming from our restored relationship with Father God through the cross, our eternal friendship with Jesus till He returns, and our daily encounter with Him who is Holy Spirit, as our flesh is crucified. So when we actively become disciples and disciple others we open the floodgates of heaven and all is possible.

Now let's return to our barren women; either you believe the lie of the enemy and stay locked in your barrenness, confined to the barracks of church, or you choose to believe God. Faith is the absolute essential of discipleship, and seeing things with the eyes of faith unlocks the bounty of God's kingdom. You can be a spiritual mum or dad – yes, *you!* For God does not see barrenness but fruitfulness and many children. You can mother or father a new generation for Jesus. It will be costly, demanding, time consuming, but it will be the best thing you have ever had the privilege to do. It will require you to share your life, your home, and your family. For Lorna and me it has meant caring for many as part of our extended family: Rachel in St Helens, Mark in Newham, Liz in Newham, Mandy in Hastings, Tom in Guildford, Ruth, Michelle and Laura in Newcastle. These and others whom we have fathered or mothered have become lifelong friends, and now we pray also for their children.

This brings us finally to the prime task of parents: babies! In this case it's spiritual babies. Again, with the gift of faith we need to ask the Lord to give us a special burden for someone's salvation. (It would usually be someone we know and have a growing relationship with; for some of us it could be one of our own physical children.) Take that person to the Throne of Grace daily and agree together with other believers for their salvation – maybe in a prayer triplet – then develop a faith picture of them following Christ, even of them being baptised. Conceiving spiritual babies is not only possible; by the grace of God *it works.* It does, however, bring yet more spiritual and parental responsibility!

Remember: it's not over till the barren woman sings!

Acorns to oak trees: 3 steps towards mature discipleship

- Why not find three or four other men or women and form an Accountability Group as described? It could be a springboard to so much more!
- Do you have a spare room in your home? Could you offer it to a new Christian? Hospitality flows from disciples.
- Continue, whether they are Christians or not, to pray for your own children, grandchildren, and for the generations to come.

CHAPTER FOUR

It is being transformed by grace

Revelation 3:12
The one who is victorious I will make a pillar in the temple of my God. Never again will they leave it. I will write on them the name of my God and the name of the city of my God, the new Jerusalem, which is coming down out of heaven from my God; and I will also write on them my new name.

The goal of discipleship is nothing short of utter transformation into the image of Christ. John the Baptist's stated desire 'He must become greater and I must become less' (John 3:30) is surely a shared goal for all disciples. How this transformation takes place in every soul is different, but the common denominator is grace – amazing, outrageous, wonderful – flowing from the cross. It is within such communities of grace that transformation takes place and transformed souls emerge. Such is the Body of Christ – Church with ragged edges – even for those starting a journey towards transformation but still some distance from salvation. 'Belonging before believing' marks it out; *all* are welcome into such a community.

Let's be honest...

Many congregations just aren't grace communities anymore. They have battened down the spiritual hatches, pulled up the spiritual drawbridge and sought to protect themselves from the wicked and changing world beyond their doors. There is an insistence that you have to believe before you can belong, and believe in a way that they do, as difference is challenging and unsettling. Sadly many of us have believed the lies of the enemy that our lives won't ever get any better, and that a kind of twilight zone Christianity is as good as it gets. We have also slipped into a works-based Christianity foreign to the pages of the New Testament, and the enemy's treadmill has squeezed our spiritual life into a hugely constraining box marked 'Sunday Service'. The work of the Lord has come before the Lord of the work.

How can we change?

Well, let's look at some transformed souls to encourage and instruct us: Simon (meaning 'Reed') became Peter (meaning 'Rock') – a three-year transformation in which most of us can see reflections. John (one of the 'sons of thunder') became John ('the disciple whom Jesus loved', who embodied love) – a thirty-year transformation that should encourage even the hardest soul! Saul (angry persecutor) became Paul (apostle to the Gentiles, passionate evangelist) – a ten-year journey including at least three years in Arabia, which encourages us all to continue praying for even the hardest of hearts. I am sure all three would have said they were still 'a work in progress'! I began as an insecure young man with low self-esteem but am being transformed year by year into David (meaning 'Beloved of God') – a journey which has taken thirty-nine years thus far! So there's hope for you all!

Let's observe the common strands from these four examples:

- Each of them took time – no overnight miracles here.
- Each happened in the context of the community of those who follow Jesus.
- Each was in essence a work of the soul. Their personality remained unchanged; it was however profoundly sanctified.
- The crucial tipping point was being filled with the Holy Spirit. He gave them the grace and character needed to journey forward to full salvation.

The 'overcomer' mentioned frequently in Revelation is the archetype transformed soul whose life has been woven into the fabric of the New Jerusalem – a goal we all should covet and aim for, but one we will not fully reach this side of eternity. Discipleship is the route you and I travel on this transformative journey, and it's important that we choose our travelling companions well.

2 Corinthians 11:2-3
I am jealous for you with a godly jealousy. I promised you to one husband, to Christ, so that I might present you as a pure virgin to him. But I am afraid that just as Eve was deceived by the serpent's cunning, your minds may somehow be led astray from your sincere and pure devotion to Christ.

Paul's words here are addressed to the Church at Corinth, which was made up of disciples. Today we too need to keep our discipleship Jesus-centred rather than church-centred, and we need to understand and act as the Body of Christ, Jesus' church, with its infinite variety, flavour and colour. We don't need to protect the Church; in fact we should actively encourage its ragged edges as people at all different stages seek to draw closer to this community of grace.

A favourite phrase Christians often use today is that they are 'a work in progress' – a reasonable description, if it's true. *Progress* seems to be the crucial word; if we are continually messing up and not learning or moving forward as a result, we are not 'a work in progress'! We need to understand that the battleground of transformation is our soul and give it our full attention. Paul in one of his superb blessings makes this distinction:

1 Thessalonians 5:23
May your whole spirit, soul and body be kept blameless at the coming of our Lord Jesus Christ.

Our spirit is born again at the point of conversion. Then begins the work of salvation (Philippians 2:12b) in our soul – our mind, will and emotions – and finally this translates into our body, which we look after well, and it becomes 'a temple of the Holy Spirit' (1 Corinthians 6:19). The battle for our soul is relentless, but we have the Holy Spirit as our helper. Our minds are assailed in all kinds of ways: what we see, what we hear, what we read. However, with God's help we choose the mind of Christ. Our wills are like a reed bed being pulled in so many directions. However, with God's help we say, 'Your will be done. Your Kingdom come.' Our emotions can wildly fluctuate and be a most unhelpful spiritual barometer. However, with God's help we choose to weep about those things that break God's heart and rejoice when people reach the full potential of the humanity God intended for them.

We need, in this glorious process of transformation, to stoke the boiler of our soul. Soul food includes regular Holy Spirit top-ups, believing prayer, standing on God's promises, exercising faith, witnessing to Christ and much more. God is on our side in this great endeavour: Jesus is the lover of my soul; the Great Shepherd is the restorer of my soul. If we don't look after our soul the enemy will attack, so discipling needs to focus in on what is going on in a person's soul – 'Why, my soul, are you downcast?' (Psalm 42:11) – and we need to speak to our souls – 'Praise the LORD, O my soul.' (Psalm 103:1a).

I've always been impressed with Paul's honesty in Romans 7; for the first six chapters of Romans he sets out the whole gospel in a way that thrills and challenges, and then in Chapter 7 he honestly says, 'I'm struggling!' He wants to do one thing (the good) but ends up doing another (the bad) – it's the classic flesh versus Spirit battle.

> Romans 7:24
> *What a wretched man I am! Who will rescue me from this body that is subject to death?*

The answer he gives comes loud and clear in Romans 8 and beyond: the Holy Spirit makes all the difference and grace is sufficient! So you too can be transformed by grace and in the power of the Holy Spirit. You too can become a living testimony of the power of the gospel. It's never too late.

Annie was seventy when she became a Christian. She lived in a tower block in Wakefield and had always been a very private person, but in short, becoming a Christian utterly changed her life. She systematically evangelised her block of flats helping some twenty folk to become Christians, and she became an elder in her local congregation at age seventy-three!

Your transformation and helping another soul in their transformation can open the door to many others and successive generations finding the Saviour.

Acorns to oak trees: 3 steps towards mature discipleship

- Look for a fresh encounter with the Holy Spirit that you might progress from one degree of glory to another (2 Corinthians 3:18).
- Recommit yourself to the company of those who follow in 'The Way' and let others speak into your life.
- Look for a congregation with 'ragged edges' so you are constantly surrounded by those more mature (being woven) and those seeking a relationship with Jesus Christ.

Chapter Five

It is solved by walking with God

'Solvitur ambulando,'[15] said Augustine of Hippo; I would add, 'cum Deo'[16]. I am utterly convinced that the Lord is as much, or even more, concerned about the quality of our journey or pilgrimage, as He is about about our arrival at the finishing line. There is no pattern for our journey as all are unique, but some principles are transferable: on the job training is essential and there is no standing still. We are to see each person as a divine encounter, be in constant contact with HQ, and commit each day to Him.

In Genesis, God walks in the garden with Adam and Eve (3:8), then Enoch, Noah, Laban, Abraham and Isaac are all described as having 'walked with God' (5:22, 6:9, 24:40, 48:15). Abraham's servant also acknowledges: '...As for me the LORD has led me on the journey...' (24:27). Are we giving enough attention to our walk with God, or is that one reason why we feel embarrassed by the thought of discipling others? Kosuke Koyama says of the disciples:

> ...they learned the word of God in the wilderness as they walked 3 miles an hour with the 3 mile an hour God.[17]

Our souls just refuse to travel at speed. Do we need to slow down and pay more attention to the Master? Do we need to try and do less in our lives and hence achieve more?

---

[15] 'It is solved by walking'
[16] 'with God'
[17] *Three Mile an Hour God: Biblical reflections;* Maryknoll, N.Y.; Orbis (1979) page 7.

1 Peter 3:18 (MSG)
Your life is a journey you must travel with a deep consciousness of God.

Walking is both mobile but also slow enough for us to take in what God wants to show us. Certainly my physical walk slowed me down and opened me up afresh to listening, seeing, feeling, and touching deeply His creation and His heart of love for humanity. Precious times! Interestingly, Street Pastors do a 'slow walk' as they bring God's presence to the streets.

Let's be honest...

As a pastor and mature Christian who should know better I am constantly trying to do too much and believing that through more activity things will get better, the Church will grow, and people will find Christ – all done with the best of intentions, but all to no avail. When will I learn that one word delivered to another soul from God is better than a thousand from me; that time spent discipling another guy is always worth more than hours in endless talk shops; and that investment in mission-focused unity projects will always produce more than an individual congregation's efforts? Over thirty-one years I have seen sincere, loving believers trying to keep too many balls in the air and frustrating themselves, terrorised by the demands of their congregations; having their Sundays stressed by competing expectations; and in the end heading off for one of the new churches believing all will be different.

How can we change?

So what's your spiritual speedometer saying? Surely there is no other solution but to confess that our journey has stalled and that our attempt to race ahead has left us badly exposed to the enemy's attacks and taunts.

1 John 2:6
Whoever claims to live in him must live as Jesus did.

We must dispense with the temptation to go faster and the arrogance that suggests to us that we know a better way. We must throw off those things which would hold us back or slow us down: physical and spiritual. 'On the job training' is the Jesus model; as He walked, He talked, He taught, He used metaphors and stories, and He responded to people's needs as He encountered them, always being prepared for the interruption (Mark 5). Psalm 84 is one of my favourites and has become known as the Pilgrim's Psalm.

> **Psalm 84:5**
> *Blessed are those whose strength is in you, whose hearts are set on pilgrimage.*

Walking with God is a clear choice we need to make daily. It's never an easy choice as it is costly and will take us into 'desert places' but we carry in us transformation and good news, which will be received often and gladly by the neediest. So as you walk, commit each day to the One who truly holds it and all its surprises in the palm of His Hand. See each person you encounter as a divine appointment: hear God, receive His direction, and bless them with the Shalom of Christ. As you journey, be in constant communion with the Throne of Grace.

Now, not all of us can undertake a pilgrimage or a long walk, but all of us can have the heart of a pilgrim. Prayer walking our streets, neighbourhood, and city is a crucial ministry. I remember the example of Richard Seals in Guildford who, as a regular prayer walker, challenged me in this area.

You can be a secret pastor to your street. Walking the streets of our cities, as Street Pastors, is not just a mercy ministry to inebriated young people, it's a sign of the compassion of Jesus for the lost. In the 1980s, Graham Kendrick and others encouraged us to March for Jesus where we were. His song 'We'll Walk the Land' (shown opposite) is, and remains, a prophetic call to disciples today.

If only we would walk our land again with hearts on fire. Let it be so again in our generation! Daniel Cozens' 'Walk of 1000 Men' doesn't claim pilgrimage status, but it does mobilise us to do just that.[18]

---

[18] See www.throughfaithmissions.org

We'll Walk the Land[19]

We'll walk the Land with hearts on fire
And every step will be a prayer
Hope is rising, new day dawning
Sound of singing fills the air

Let the flame burn brighter
In the heart of the darkness
Turning night to glorious day
Let the song grow louder
Let our love grow stronger
Let it shine, let it shine

Acorns to oak trees: 3 steps towards mature discipleship

- Why not take responsibility for an area, maybe even for your street, and regularly prayer walk it?
- Let me challenge you to develop a pilgrim spirit: read 'Pilgrim' by J. John (a contemporary retelling of Pilgrim's Progress).
- Why not mobilise your community to March for Jesus once again?

---

[19] Graham Kendrick (c) 1989 Make Way Music.
www.grahamkendrick.co.uk

CHAPTER SIX

It is ignited by graces and gifts

There is no doubt, and plenty of evidence, as to who made the difference to those first disciples – the twelve, the band of women, and many others; 120 in all – waiting and praying in the upper room prior to the Pentecostal birthday of the church. It was the Holy Spirit. Just as Jesus had promised, He had come, and – wow! – He had changed everything. A mighty wind had blown away the clouds so that religious practice, tradition and law could be seen in their proper place – totally subservient to grace, faith and power in the Holy Spirit. Tongues of fire had brought cleansing and renewal, and made them into holy channels through which heaven could be poured to earth. Fearful followers had become faith-filled disciples, and on that one day three thousand souls had been ushered into the kingdom, all filled with that same Holy Spirit. Pre-Pentecost hidden discipleship was no longer; post-Pentecost public discipleship was at the heart of this new movement. Notice that Acts never shows the disciples as *intentionally* creating church; they simply reached others with the gospel and then discipled them, and the cycle continued. Local churches (in a city or a town) were simply an organisational necessity as the numbers grew. The Holy Spirit helped in this glorious process by producing in them graces (fruit) and giving them access to tools to help them replicate the ministry of Jesus (gifts).

Let's be honest…

The Holy Spirit was hardly mentioned in the congregation I grew up in, and, when 'it' was, 'it' was called 'the Holy Ghost', conjuring up all kinds of scary pictures in the mind of a young boy! We called ourselves Trinitarian but only mentioned Father and Son. On a wider stage the Church in the UK did not know how to respond to the birth of Pentecostalism in 1905 in Los Angeles, USA, and so choose to marginalise and ignore it (now it accounts for 25% of Christendom). In the 1960's the Fountains Trust sought to bring the Holy Spirit to the mainline churches, and this was followed by the charismatic renewal and the birth of new congregations, initially called house churches. The rest, as they say, is history, but suffice it to say that it resulted in confusion for many Christians. Poor leadership either left the Holy Spirit as mystery or failed to explain what biblically was being experienced, and that, in my judgment, is why much of the strength of the classic denominations in the UK was lost In general, since then, evangelicals have judged the rest of the Church, and liberals have pushed the rest of the Church away; both have been the losers and the UK church has been hugely damaged in the process. None of this was the work of the Holy Spirit; on the contrary, it was a fleshly response often from pride-filled leaders wanting to remain in control.

How can we change?

Well firstly we all need to repent of the mess we have either got into or allowed the UK church to get into. Then we need to cry out to God to have mercy and allow us another opportunity to get this right; for the future salvation of our nation and its missionary potential are on the line.

Then we need to disciple a new generation into an understanding of the person and work of the Holy Spirit. We need to help them receive His fruit into their lives: one fruit with nine named flavours which mirror the very person and character of Jesus: love, joy, peace, patience, kindness, gentleness, goodness, faithfulness, and self-control. This fruit is not separate from Jesus; it is in essence the very nature of Christ, for each aspect can be found completely in Him. The Holy Spirit reflects the absolute holiness of God and creates in you and me holy channels to pour through these core values of what it means to be fully human, made in the image of God. These values are to enable Christ to increase and self to decrease; they are to form in you and me the character of Jesus. Disciples' lives are like a canvas upon which gradually emerges the image of Jesus.

From the Acorn of Discipleship...

In my experience, character is as important as charisma in the use of the gifts. Without such character, catastrophe follows. So this Holy Spirit fruit gives us the character we need to correctly handle the gifts He gives and minister well in Jesus' name.

Having the fruit in place and the holy channel flowing, we are then ready to open ourselves up to the gifts that the Holy Spirit makes available to us. These are like the tool kit of our discipleship and help us exercise the continuing ministry of Jesus today. In essence we encourage one another as disciples to trust the Master that whenever we are directed to step out in faith and do the things Jesus did, just like He promised we would (John 14:12), the gifts are released (down the holy channel) in the moment of usefulness. They are not our possession as disciples (so we can't say we are a healer) and they remain God's gifts, channelled through our lives, to the point of need; thus the ministry of Jesus continues through us. Of the nine gifts – wisdom, word of knowledge, faith, healing, discernment, miraculous powers, prophecy, tongues, and their interpretation – all uniquely have their place but perhaps three are worth commenting on.

DISCERNMENT

This is an essential part of discipleship: 'What is Holy Spirit and what is not?' is a vital question. With more discernment the Body of Christ would not be led down so many blind spiritual alleys.

FAITH

> **Hebrews 11:6**
> *...without faith it is impossible to please God...*

All disciples must live by faith and know the language of faith. Faith needs to return to the heart of the Body of Christ in the UK before reformation and transformation can truly happen.

WISDOM

Origen (one of the Early Church Fathers) said:

> *Travellers in the road to God's wisdom find that the further they go, the more the road opens out until it stretches to infinity.*

And how much we need God's wisdom today to chart a way forward for the Body of Christ.

It goes without saying that the greatest of all the gifts is that of salvation: full and free. Of course, graces and gifts and all the Holy Spirit has to bring to us as individual disciples and to the church need to be carefully and wisely received, and that's where the discipleship comes in, giving the person being discipled not only teaching but practical wisdom and testimony of how and when the gifts are used. Remember that in 1 Corinthians 14 Paul reminds us that the gifts must only ever be used in the context of, and for the upbuilding and edification of, the Body of Christ.

I feel a bit like I am trailing the 'Six Million Dollar Man': 'Gentlemen, we can rebuild him. We have the technology. We have the capability to create the world's first bionic man!' But seriously, we do need to rebuild the Body of Christ in the UK on a fully trinitarian foundation. We have the Gospel, we have the Holy Spirit, and we have Discipleship. We can take our Jesus and His gospel of grace once again to the ends of the earth!

Acorns to oak trees: 3 steps towards mature discipleship

- Go through the nine aspects of the fruit of the Spirit and check whether all are evident in equal measure in your life. If short in any area ask for help from the Lord and look for someone to 'imitate'.
- Have you exercised all nine gifts of the Spirit? If not then put yourself in a place where you might need the gift to operate and trust God!
- Put yourself on the frontline where such graces and gifts are best used and sharpened.

CHAPTER SEVEN

It is made effective by discipline

When we choose to follow Jesus and be His disciples we say goodbye to being in charge of our own life and put a notice in our personal shop window declaring 'under new management'. Put another way, if you want to come *in* (to the kingdom) you must come *under* (His lordship).

It is one thing to say, 'Jesus is Lord!' but quite another to put it into practice day by day in the fast pace of our lives. Thomas's response to Jesus in John 20:28 – 'My Lord and My God' – is probably the most complete commitment we can echo as it brings together absolute surrender to Christ with an acceptance by faith that He is the divine Son of God. Disciples are, at the core of their being, disciplined followers of Jesus, and this discipline rather than being a dry conformity is dynamic, faith-filled, foundational and an indispensable first step on which all else is built – rock rather than sand (see Matthew 7:24-27).

Let's be honest...

Today's Church in the UK could best be described as 'anything-goes Church'. As discipleship has been diminished so has any kind of discipline. We have become unbalanced in a number of key areas.

Jesus is described by John (1:14) as being full of *grace* and *truth*. We have rightly highlighted and emphasised grace and sought to purge judgemental (pharisaic) spirits as they raise their ugly heads in our midst – but as we have done this we have marginalised truth, called it fundamentalism, and forgotten that as well as embodying grace, Jesus said, 'I am ... truth' (14:6) and embodied it. A rebalancing is needed.

In declaring true worship Jesus tells us of another balance we need to maintain: *Spirit* and *truth* (4:24). We have rightly sought to update our worships styles with relevant and contemporary songs, which speak of and celebrate our relationship with God, but in doing so the casualty has often been the truth about Jesus. Whilst enjoying worshipping our God is not in itself wrong, we have in the process sacrificed aspects of the Gospel which to our sophisticated minds seem harsh and overly black and white. A rebalancing is needed.

The third area that we have become unbalanced in is *word* and *Spirit*. Either we are very much centred on God's word and wanting more and more of it, or we have allowed our focus to be almost exclusively on the Holy Spirit. Either objective truth (the Bible) or subjective truth (the Spirit), either a strong foundation built on God's word or an experiential foundation built on the Holy Spirit. But it's not an 'either or'; it's a balance that's needed for mature discipleship to flourish. Indeed the Smith Wigglesworth prophecy of 1947 about word and Spirit says as much:

> ...when these two distinct moves comes together they will be a significant step towards the renewal of the UK church.[20]

So we need to be back called into leading balanced Christian lives once again. And note that all three balances referred to include truth (personified in Jesus). Such truth, says Jesus, "will set you free" (John 8:36).

How can we change?

Hebrews 12:5-6
And have you completely forgotten this word of encouragement that addresses you as a father addresses his son? It says, 'My son, do not make light of the Lord's discipline, and do not lose heart when he rebukes you, because the Lord disciplines the one he loves, and he chastens everyone he accepts as his son.'

Disciples grow and thrive through discipline – their own and the Lord's. There are three ways in which the agenda of our lives can be set: *we* can set the agenda and be in control; if we don't, *others* (the world) will happily set the agenda for us, and we willingly or passively

---

[20] http://www.jonasclark.com/revival-history/smith-wigglesworths-rare-1947-prophecy.html

will buy into it; but for the disciple, *Jesus* is Lord, He sets the agenda, His will is what we seek, and His plan for our life is what we desire. Of course we do need to be careful not to suggest that it is all about what God does with us as a kind of puppet on a string; His Fatherly action in our lives needs to be brought together with self-control (*God-control* in the disciple) which is perhaps one of the most neglected aspects of the fruit of the Holy Spirit. In order to walk the path of discipleship we need, in a disciplined way, to embrace a Kingdom worldview, and to do this there are things that we essentially can and must do in a disciplined way. For example:

FULLY TRUST THE MASTER

He is worthy of our trust! We need an unswerving belief in His sovereignty. He sees the big picture.

> Romans 8:28
> *…in all things God works for the good of those who love him, who have been called according to his purpose.*

We choose to believe this and walk in faith even if the evidence seems to be stacking up to the contrary.

LIVE ACCORDING TO THE MAKERS INSTRUCTIONS

We choose to stand on the Word of God and believe the promises of God. We have not succumbed to a worship of the Bible for we worship the Word made flesh: Jesus. We will each day allow God's word to feed our souls, build our spirits, and be food for our journey. We look to this Living Word to direct, instruct and guide us into all truth, and we will always seek to not only be hearers of the Word but doers also.

LIVE A LIFE OF GRACE THAT POINTS PEOPLE TO JESUS

Grace is personified in Jesus and is love without strings. With the help of the Spirit we will seek to encounter people as Christ's ambassadors (2 Corinthians 5:20) and allow the Holy Spirit 'agape' channel to flow through to them so they are drawn to Jesus and find acceptance and freedom in Him. Grace communities act as both light and salt in the world.

PRAY WITHOUT CEASING

See 1 Thessalonians 5:17. Daily we need to be speaking with Father at the throne of grace, and daily He will speak to us if we have ears to hear and have learnt the art of listening. Prayer brings us into line with God's heart and will. Prayer is the bread and butter of our relationship and gives it a dynamism nothing else can. Praying in the Spirit is a special gift and grace as it utterly confuses the enemy and disarms him of any influence or power.

WORSHIPPING THE LORD

If prayer keeps us centred upon the Father, worship keeps us centred upon Jesus. Worship feeds our souls and builds trust and relationship. It includes singing songs (known and written) and new songs (unknown and from the Spirit), but can also be in the form of silence, meditation, dance, liturgy, and in any combination. The tyranny of taste can kill worship; we worship the Lord, we don't worship the worship itself. During my long walk I would be found daily on the path worshipping and singing out loud the song 'Bless The Lord O My soul (10000 reasons)' by Matt Redman.

LIVING BY FAITH

Ultimately faith is how we become a believer in Christ, a disciple, and faith is how that new relationship is sustained and deepened. Seeing things, especially people, with God's eyes is exercising faith. Standing on the sure ground of faith, as Mary did, is choosing to trust the Lord however long it takes; and even if it seems impossible, the 'but if not' faith principle (Daniel 3:18) of Shadrach, Meshach and Abednego is the disciples' default. We have burnt our worldly boats – like Columbus arriving in Scotland from Ireland – and committed our lives into His hands.

The Lord's discipline is also essential to our discipleship and ever-maturing walk. Find the perfect disciple and I will show you their imperfections, and if none seems evident there could well be an ounce of pride! The Lord disciplines us in many ways including the following:

From the Acorn of Discipleship...

HE HUMBLES US

> 1 Peter 5:5b
> ...*clothe yourselves with humility toward one another, because,*
> *'God opposes the proud but shows favor to the humble.'*

HE REBUKES US

> Revelation 3:19a
> *Those whom I love I rebuke and discipline.*

HE CALLS US TO REPENTANCE

> Revelation 3:19b
> *So be earnest and repent.*

HE HOLDS BEFORE US THE BAR OF PERFECTION

> Matthew 5:48
> *Be perfect, therefore, as your heavenly Father is perfect.*

HE REMINDS US WHERE THE SEAT OF JUDGMENT IS

> Matthew 7:1-2
> *Do not judge or you too will be judged. For in the same way you*
> *judge others you will be judged, and with the measure you use, it*
> *will be measured to you.*

The UK Church is very much like the Church in Corinth to whom Paul wrote more about discipline than any of his other churches. 'Anything-goes Church' is not found in the New Testament nor is it a place for disciples. Recently the Archbishop of Canterbury, Justin Welby, commented that every period of renewal in the life of the Body of Christ has been accompanied by a renewal of community discipline.[21] We go soft in this area of discipleship at our peril.

---

[21] See no.29 at http://www.philotrust.com/ftc/guests

Acorns to oak trees: 3 steps towards mature discipleship

- 'Therefore confess your sins to each other and pray for each other so that you may be healed.' (James 5:16a). Find a soul mate to be your confessor.
- Based on your own weaknesses decide on three things you can do in a disciplined way to help you make progress as a disciple.
- Consider the things that 'happen' to you and ask whether they might be the Lord disciplining you – and dare to ask yourself why.

CHAPTER EIGHT

It is sharpened by mission

A focus on discipleship – being and making – can seem like an inward focused internal Body of Christ activity until we remind ourselves that the early followers of Jesus in responding to the Great Commission (subsequent to Pentecost and the Holy Spirit) threw themselves wholeheartedly into their missionary calling. This was not without cost as the imprisonments of the apostles, persecution by Saul, and martyrdom of Stephen and James in Acts show. Yet these persecutions, which continued for some three hundred years, were not a cause for retreat or a ghetto mentality but the advance of the gospel. 'The blood of the martyrs [committed, active, fruitful disciples] is [truly] the seed of the Church,' said the Church Father Tertullian. Today in many parts of the world believers are still martyred for their love of Christ; indeed the China experience suggests that Tertullian's observation still remains true.

'Mission Deo' – God's rescue mission for Planet Earth – continues whether you and I are part of it or not; but I for one want my life to count for the king and His Kingdom. Paul well understood the absolute connection between mission and discipleship:

> Acts 14:21-22a
> *They preached the gospel in that city and won a large number of disciples. Then they returned to Lystra, Iconium and Antioch, strengthening the disciples and encouraging them to remain true to the faith.*

Let's be honest...

Just as discipleship has been reserved for the keen ones among us, so sadly has mission. Consequently the average believer has never been part of leading another soul to faith in Christ and conceives mission as either the preserve of para-church organisations or something that happens in distant shores. A pervasive and increasingly demanding (especially as numbers decline) institutional church culture has sucked us in and sapped the spiritual energy from us so that even if a dynamic message 'to go' touches us deeply, our zeal is quickly doused by mere religion and its duties. It's like a spiritual treadmill, and we either don't have the energy to get off or the enemy has duped our soul into a gospel of justification by works so we see no need to change or respond to the Macedonian call ('Come over and help us!'[22]) in our generation.

How can we change?

We need to refocus our lives on the one we say we follow: our Lord Jesus. When we do that we will begin to ditch the excess religious baggage and start to hear His winsome call to mission and making disciples again. It's a scary transition as we don't know where it will lead, but we do know it will break us out of our comfort zone and lead us into a life of faith and missionary endeavour. So what did Jesus say to those first disciples, Simon and Andrew?

> Mark 1:17
> *'Come, follow me,' Jesus said, 'and I will send you out to fish for people.'*

Let's look more closely at this, and hear it for ourselves, applying it to our lives. As we have previously noted, 'come' is the same Greek word translated in the Great Commission as 'go'. 'Come' is a much more attainable challenge, especially if the person saying it to us is Jesus! 'Follow me' is about remaining close to Him in every respect – physically, emotionally, spiritually, etc. – ready to receive orders from the Throne of Grace. Both suggest movement and progress, both imply the pilgrim journey, and both should be the bottom line by which we can test the authenticity of our discipleship. Standing still is no option.

---

[22] See Acts 16:9b

What would Jesus do (WWJD), what would He say, where would He be, how would He act?

Then follows a promise that if we come and if we follow Him, '[Jesus] will send [us] out to fish for people'! Context is important: Simon and Andrew were fishermen, so you and I need to interpret this for our own personal circumstance. Someone once called my first pastor, Michael, a showman, to which he responded, 'A showman for Christ.' Paul puts it this way:

> 1 Corinthians 9:22
> …*all things to all people so that by all possible means I might save some.*

Maybe you are a lorry driver and Christ would have you drive lorries into distant mission fields, or maybe you are a teacher and Christ would have you form and nurture new disciples to maturity using your teaching gift. The important emphasis is that *He* will do it, if we allow Him; we can become fruitful in our own unique mission field that He has for us (see 1 Thessalonians 5:24). It may not be fishing for men and women (personally, my fishing skills are non-existent), but He will have a unique mission assignment for you and me.

For most of us this mission assignment is to wake up to the mission-field on our own doorstep! To realise that where we spend the greatest amount of our time is probably our key mission focus and calling is a crucial revelation. For many of us this will mean our workplace, for others our place of education (school, college, university), for others the school gate, groups of mums, the guys down the pub, fellow supporters of our team, people at our leisure focus, neighbours and friendship groups, to name just a few. A tiny percentage will go on the mission field beyond our shores – and if you haven't already guessed, the UK is now a mission-field in its own right. Fewer will become paid Church leaders and will have to be very focused to keep following Jesus and equipping the saints for work of ministry (Ephesians 4:12). Personally, the sooner we return to church leaders who are not full time but 'tent-making' the better. Most effective missionary work is done by the nameless ones – 'idiotes' in the Greek (Acts 8:1-4, 1 Corinthians 4:10) – those scattered fools for Christ!

And what did Paul have to say about this task, out of his missionary and discipling experience?

2 Corinthians 5:20
We are therefore Christ's ambassadors, as though God were making his appeal through us.

Ambassadors are sent to foreign lands to represent the Monarch and the Government; so as disciples we are not called to hide away in ghettos or holy places but to be the presence of Jesus in the world, salt to savour what is good, and light to pierce the darkness. The context of Paul's description is that we need to be out there embodying the Gospel of reconciliation calling men and women back to God, and being active peacemakers among warring humanity. Peter also refers to the size of this missionary task by describing us as 'foreigners and exiles' (1 Peter 2:11), echoing Jesus' words that, 'In this world you will have trouble. But take heart! I have overcome the world.' (John 16:33b).

Disciples are missionaries and missionaries are disciples. It's not one or the other, it's 'both and', two sides of the same coin of being a follower of Jesus today. Without discipleship we will reach the multitudes but gradually lose them back to the world. Without mission we will have a faulty, incomplete experience of discipleship and create a puffed up pharisaic elite that will seek to justify themselves and keep the world at bay.

Acorns to oak trees: 3 steps towards mature discipleship

- Replay in your heart the call from Jesus to follow, and hear afresh the mission-field He has prepared for you.
- Draw up a relational tree of those you are in regular contact with, who are not as yet Christians. Form a prayer triplet to agree together for their salvation.
- Seek an experience of a mission-field unfamiliar to you to increase your first-hand experience of God at work.

CHAPTER NINE

It is how we live our lives!

John Stott, in his final book 'The Radical Disciple', lists eight aspects of effective discipleship born out of a lifetime of trying to follow Christ; at number five he has 'simplicity'. At an International Consultation held in the UK in March 1980 a challenge to the whole church called the 'Evangelical Commitment to Simple Lifestyle'[23] was issued. Sadly it was, and has continued to be, almost ignored, but I believe its time has now come. Let me remind you of its essential emphases:

> *1. **The New Community:** we rejoice that the church is intended to be God's new community, which exhibits new values, new standards and a new lifestyle.*

> *2. **Personal Lifestyle:** we lay down no rules or regulations, but in view of the fact that about 10,000 people die of starvation every day, we determine to simplify our lifestyle.*

> *3. **International development:** we are shocked by the poverty of millions and resolve to contribute more generously to human development projects. But government action is essential.*

> *4. **Justice and politics:** we believe that the present situation of social injustice is abhorrent to God and that change can and must come.*

> *5. **Evangelism:** we are deeply concerned for the vast millions of unevangelized peoples. The call to a simple lifestyle must not be divorced from the call to be a responsible witness.*

---

[23] http://www.lausanne.org/en/documents/lops/77-lop-20.html

> 6. **The Lord's return:** *we believe that when Jesus returns, those who have ministered to Him by ministering to the least will be saved, for the reality of saving faith is exhibited in serving love.*

I feel deep down that thirty-four years on this call is as relevant if not more so.

Let's be honest…

Most of us live anything but simple lives, and as a result we are oppressed in our souls by multiple temptations around us to sustain a worldly lifestyle which we think will help us be acceptable to, and fit in with, those around us. This must be one of the chief contributing factors to our declining influence and numerical strength as the Body of Christ in the UK: well-meaning atheists are indistinguishable from so-called Christians.

How can we change?

The call to discipleship embraces a call to a simple lifestyle. We are called to the modern equivalents of poverty, chastity and obedience; to go against the flow, and to make cross-shaped stands wherever and whenever our Lord leads us to do so. At the heart of our call is the call to community, to holding all things in common (Acts 4:32) and giving to anyone as you see their needs (2:46). Part of my formation as a disciple is instructive here. We were part of a work of God in London's East End in the late 1980s; faced as we were with poverty on a scale we had not experienced before, and set in a multi-cultural, multi-faith context, we were impelled by the Holy Spirit to create a community based on Acts 2:42-47. From this flowed a radical sharing of possessions and goods and a creation of many shared households where new Christians learnt to be disciples. From small beginnings 'Shoulder to Shoulder Employment Project' was launched and helped many into or back into work through simple life skills. 'Together we Can' was an attempt by suburban churches to support us in this work and resulted in many being blessed with basic needs, even to the extent of furnishing a new home. Personally it led us to share our home; lodgers short and long term became part of our extended family, our washing machine was used for far more than our own household, and we learnt to stop holding onto things we no longer used or needed. I recall the Lord testing our hearts in this area when in 1988 we were visiting door to door in a local tower block and encountered a family who were struggling to survive and had succumbed to borrowing £500 from a local loan shark. They were paying £32 per week back just in interest - echoes of the experience of many today! As we prayed about their situation, the Lord reminded us of the only savings we had: £500 for a family holiday the next summer. The short story is that I spent a particularly frightening evening at the back of an East End pub (with dog collar on) paying off this debt and daring to ask a very scary looking man for a receipt! The whole family have since thrived and the parents become Christians. A month later a letter arrived from a lady in Basingstoke we did not know. She wrote: 'The Lord told me of you, and I found your contact details through the URC. The Lord told me to send you a cheque for £500. Be blessed!' Faith-building or what! Part of me would like to put believers in a spiritual 'tardis' and take them for a season into a place radically different than their own setting, as this would be worth far more than a hundred lectures on simple lifestyle.

I wonder if all these issues – lifestyle, evangelism, mission, spiritual parenting, transformation, walking with God, receiving His graces and gifts, being disciplined and truly the Body of Christ – hinge upon our faith and trust in Christ. I have found that there is no room for manoeuvre here as it's either total or subject to chipping away by our own desperate clinging to control or the enemy exploiting our many weaknesses. Perhaps I could finish by giving you my ten own personal aspirational lifestyle statements to lead us closer to Christ.

- Live within your income, and don't borrow money or live on credit. The one exception is probably a mortgage, but don't take out one that is too large.
- Sponsor a child in a developing world country and pray for them.
- Stand up for the poor and dispossessed, and campaign on their behalf via your MP, Parliament and other avenues open to you.
- Keep your possessions to a minimum; travel light. When you can give away things to bless others, do so but don't trumpet it.
- Tithe into the storehouse, the church, and then actively ensure the congregation is wisely directing its resources into discipleship and mission and not just buildings.

- Adopt a family in your congregation to encourage and bless, or do the same with someone who is single.
- Create a household altar: a place where either individually or collectively the household can speak to and hear from the Lord.
- Consider how you are spending your money over a period of a month and ask the question whether that pattern needs to change.
- Remember to bless your family relations even if you don't see them much or they don't know Christ. Be generous towards them and pray for them.
- In a non-judgemental and natural way make Jesus clearly the centre of your lives, household and world.

Acorns to oak trees: 3 steps towards mature discipleship

- Ask whether your life looks discernable different from those around you? What can you do to simplify how you live?
- Hold a garage sale of all that is surplus in your household and give the money raised to a project which will make a difference in the lives of others either here in the UK or overseas.
- Pray about how you live your life and how you spend your income, and see what the Lord says to you.

CHAPTER TEN

It can't survive in the upper room of religion

Easter encapsulates the call to discipleship. Good Friday is the most significant day of the Christian year for without the cross there can be no resurrection.

> *On the mount of crucifixion*
> *Fountains open deep and wide;*
> *Through the floodgates of God's mercy*
> *Flowed a vast and gracious tide*
> *Grace and love, like mighty rivers*
> *Poured incessant from above*
> *And heavens peace and perfect justice*
> *Kissed a guilty world in love.*
>
> *William Rees (1802-1883)*

This verse of a hymn beautifully summarises the work of Calvary. Jesus chose in obedience to His Father to die for the sins of Planet Earth. Personally He died for me! Alleluia! Discipleship at its purest means to follow Jesus, thus fully entering into His death. Our baptism itself does not directly achieve salvation or create discipleship; it is our act of obedience that publicly evidences and seals it, but do we see this in the way that those first Christians saw it? Paul says, '...I no longer live, but Christ lives in me...' (Galatians 2:20), 'For me, to live is Christ and to die is gain' (Philippians 1:21), and '...if anyone is in Christ, the new creation has come: The old has gone, the new is here!' (2 Corinthians 5:17). How serious are we and prepared to die to self and live for Jesus? He offers no halfway house (Matthew 16:24-25). Please, let's avoid cheap grace!

Two days later the story of Easter Sunday unfolds: Christ is risen! He is risen indeed! Alleluia! On that hinge-of-history day Thomas, the disciple who doubted, eventually affirmed, 'My Lord and my God' (John 20:28). 'OMG' seems to be a popular exclamation or text speak for something new, fresh, out of the box, or unexpected. Brought face to face with the living risen Christ, 'OMG' is a start, but discipleship goes beyond that orthodox statement of the divinity of Christ. Disciples choose to make Him Lord of every aspect of their lives, relationships and future. They also need actively, in His risen power, to declare Jesus is Lord by faith over people, situations, and even nations!

Let's be honest...

The Saturday between Good Friday and Easter Sunday is the place where discipleship can hit the buffers of religion! Salvation emphasises that Jesus died for my messed up life and me. The danger is, then, that because of a lack of discipline, we are left in the cosy, closed upper room of religion. You feel clean, want to start to live His new life, yet because no one shows you how and walks with you (especially in those first crucial days/months of faith), you default to a religious zealot: too heavenly minded to be of any earthy good. Those precious souls you prayed into the kingdom, whom Jesus paid the price for, snatched back into a mere upper room '...form of godliness but denying its power...' (2 Timothy 3:5) is a tragedy with eternal consequences. Staying in the upper room is the slippery slope to powerless religion that helps no one. Make no mistake, religion is man-made whilst faith is a gift.

How can we change?

By moving! From the Cross to the Resurrection and on to mature discipleship. Disciples learn quickly by doing and moving: living in the power of His Resurrection (Philippians 3:10), living by faith (Hebrews 11:1/6), and sharing the good news that Jesus is risen and alive today! The first disciples risked all for Jesus and the Gospel, and we are called to do no less. Our tendency to place unspoken limits in our response to what we will be prepared to do and say for Christ leaves us in the badly exposed place between religion and faith, and the enemy rubs his hands in glee. So how did those first disciples make real their cross-shaped faith in the risen Christ, and how is this instructive for us today?

- They worked it out as an emerging community of faith. They were more often than not together (John 20:19,26,30; 21:2; Acts 1:6,14; 2:1). Faith is not worked out in an individualistic way but as a community. We would do well to re-engage with the whole Body of Christ.
- The band of women that had also followed Jesus and tended especially to his physical needs were very much part of this community, and the disciples clearly honoured and included them (John 20:1,11,18; Acts 1:14-15; 2:1,41). Therefore we should recognise the unique contributions brought by both men and women equally to the whole Body of Christ.
- Whilst fear was an ever present reality (John 20:19) they chose to trust God and receive from Jesus the necessary reassurance, shalom, Holy Spirit and revelation necessary for the journey ahead. We too must trust the only one truly worthy of our trust – 'Trust and obey, there's no other way'[24]
- The call to discipleship was never far away, so in Galilee by the lake Jesus reminds them that He alone brings the harvest (John 21:6), meets their needs (21:12-13), and reminds them of their prime task: to feed and love his lambs/sheep (21:15-17), and to follow him alone (21:19). There, in these final words of Jesus, is our mission: *win, consolidate, disciple, send.* We would do well to make them our own experience.
- They waited, they prayed, and they honoured godly leadership (Acts 1:4,14,24-26). We would do well to imitate them today; we have forgotten that patience is ours through the fruit of the Spirit, that 'God does nothing but in answer to prayer' (John Wesley), and that godly leadership is crucial to any godly endeavour.

So don't allow your faith to hit the upper room buffers and don't sell those short you are spiritually responsible for and should be discipling by not telling them of our Easter Sunday faith!

---

[24] *When we walk with the Lord;* John Henry Sammis (1846-1919)

Acorns to oak trees: 3 steps towards mature discipleship

- Return to the Cross and ensure you fully understand its enduring power and magnetism. Read 'The Cross of Christ' by John Stott (1986).
- Fast forward to the Resurrection and touch its power: read 'Who Moved the Stone' by Frank Morrison (1987)
- Resolve to be more trusting and interactive with the community of believers Christ has joined you to.

CONCLUSION

A call to reform the Oak Tree of the Body of Christ.

Jeremiah 6:16
...Stand at the crossroads and look; ask for the ancient paths, ask where the good way is, and walk in it, and you will find rest for your souls...

At a crossroads we definitely are, as the Body of Christ in the UK, and clear leadership and direction from the Lord is necessary, if we are to walk and find rest. 'Ancient paths' are the key. Solomon's assertion in Ecclesiastes 1:9-11 that '...there is nothing new under the sun...' is a truth we need to hear afresh. We could all do with taking some time out to read the accounts of saints who over the past two millennia learnt to live in the light of His presence (for instance, St. Cuthbert, St. Augustine, Teresa of Avila, Bernard of Clairaux, Julian of Norwich, Dietrich Bonhoeffer, C.S. Lewis).

We are in the midst of seeing one of the most fundamental periods of reformation in the structure and nature of the church here in the UK, a spiritual earthquake reminiscent of the profound changes set in motion during the Evangelical Revival. The great preachers of that time, John Wesley and George Whitfield, took the Gospel to ordinary people in a relevant life-changing way. What Wesley also did was to have a method as old as the Great Commission called 'Making Disciples'. Prior to Methodism, the 18th century Church had, as its primary message, 'Come!' The Church leaders 'did ministry', the ordinary members were passive, and the focus was the Sunday meeting. Sound familiar? John Wesley created change. He instigated a new way of being church where the primary emphasis was, 'Go!' The ministry was done by the leaders *and* the laity, the ordinary members no longer passive but being disciples; the message was holistic, and the Church in the big and in the small served it. This created a mobilised Church that saw change happen in the world of business and education, and church attendance increased. *From the acorn of discipleship...*

We are in a new chapter of the Church characterised by breakout! We have realised that we must break out of our buildings (many of which are no longer fit for purpose), break out of our ghetto mentality (going back out onto the streets and amongst our neighbours), and break out of our 'religious rut' (practice, language and Sunday focus). We have begun by experimenting with new ways of worship (Cafe Church, Messy Church, etc.), new ways of meeting needs (Food Banks, CAP Centres, Parenting Courses) and new opportunities to take grace onto the streets (Street Pastors, Healing on the Streets). Above all we have discovered afresh that we need to be a Jesus people (a Grace Community) doing the things He did (meeting people where they are) and touching lives with heaven's blessing (acts of kindness and attitudes just like Him – see Matthew 5:1-10 and Philippians 2:5). *From the acorn of discipleship...*

We need a new generation of faith-filled leaders who are prepared to call time on the structures and patterns of life which have become unfit for purpose, and create new ways of being church. Such a generation will need wise mentors to support and guide them, new vision to shape the journey they and God's people will take, and be uncluttered with extraneous surplus institutional or religious baggage. Leaders of denominations or streams will need to protect them and be 100% behind them as they pioneer these new ways and usher in a new chapter of faith and growth for the church in the UK. *From the acorn of discipleship...*

Above all, this is a grass roots, local church, upwards agenda for change which will need to be resourced, responded to, and will radically alter central church structures and bring agendas back to mission and discipleship.

So finally allow me to dream of what such a church might look like in the UK:

- I dream of a church full of passionate fruitful mature disciples.
- I dream of a church where every believer is mobilised and doing the stuff Jesus did.
- I dream of a church that the world can't ignore because it embodies a different kingdom.
- I dream of a church which has a bias to the poor, the marginalised and those the world has discarded, and blesses the rich to serve them.
- I dream of a church, ever expansive, with ragged edges, where we leave our Jesus to do the building.
- I dream of a church that chooses to go into the dark places, light a candle, and say to the world, 'We beg to differ in Jesus' name.'
- I dream of a church full of every generation, an intergenerational family whose welcome encompasses all.
- I dream of a church which bears no name except the name of Jesus.

May your dreams and mine by realised as we allow Jesus, Lord of the Church, to reform us. May each of us become all we were always meant to be as disciples of Jesus. May the acorns of our lives be buried with Him, and together come to create afresh the Oak Tree of the Body of Christ in our day and generation.

From the acorn of discipleship...

Bibliography

Food for the journey

During my years preparation for Sabbatical I have been blessed by reading the following books and, as you have seen, have quoted from some of them.

Discipleship; David Watson; Hodder & Stoughton (1981)

Disciple; Juan Carlos Ortiz; Lakeland (1975)

Spiritual Discipleship; J Oswald Sanders; Moody (1990)

The Journey; Alistair McGrath; Hodder & Stoughton (1999)

The Great Omission; Dallas Willard; Monarch (2006)

The Way is made by Walking; Arthur Paul Boers; IVP (2007)

The Radical Disciple; John Stott; IVP (2010)

Lost Heritage; Kim Tan; Highland (1996)

Pilgrim; J John; Philo Trust (2012)

Pilgrimage; Ian Bradley; Lion (2009)

Lessons in Discipleship: Hudson Taylor; Roger Steer; Monarch (1995)

If you want to walk on water you've got to get out of the boat; John Ortberg; Zondervan (2001)

Radical; David Platt; Multnomah (2010)

Follow Me; David Platt; Tyndale (2013)